My First Book about the Ocean Alphabet

Amazing Animal Books
Children's Picture Books

By Molly Davidson

Mendon Cottage Books
JD-Biz Corp Publishing

Download Free Books!
http://MendonCottageBooks.com

Read More Amazing Animal Books

Purchase at Amazon.com

. **Download Free Books!**

http://MendonCottageBooks.com

 is for an Australian Sea Lion

They live on the shores of South Australia.

They have two layers of fur to help keep them warm in cold water.

 **B** is for the Blue Ringed Octopus

Elias Levy © Wikimedia Commons

Blue ringed octopuses are only about 8 cm long.

They live in the oceans from Japan to Australia.

C is for the Coral Reef

The coral reef is a home and a food source for 25% of all ocean life.

Some coral reefs are as old as 10,000 years!

D

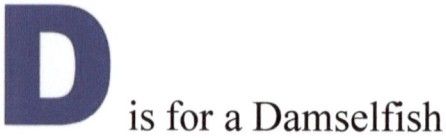 is for a Damselfish

They can 14 inches long, and all the species are brightly colored.

They live mostly in coral reefs and some live off the coast of southern California and Mexico.

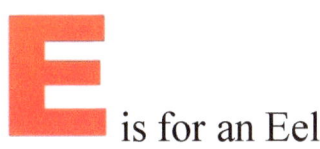 is for an Eel

Blue Eel

Eels can grow as long as 13 feet, and weigh as much as 55 pounds.

Eels live in shallow ocean water, and burrow in the mud, rocks, and sand.

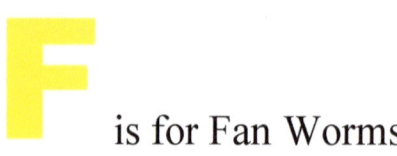

F is for Fan Worms

Fan worms attach to the sand and the rocks.

They use their many tentacles to filter through passing ocean water for food.

They can pull all their tentacles inside, if they think a fish is coming to chew on them.

G
is for a Green Turtle

Brocken Inaglory © Wikimedia Commons

Green turtles are one of the largest species of turtle, weighing up to 700 pounds.

H  is for a Hammerhead Shark

Hammerheads swim in groups during the day, and hunt alone at night.

Hammerheads have eyes on the side of their head so they can see in all directions, all the time.

I is for an Indo-Pacific Bottlenose Dolphin

Dinkum © Wikimedia Commons

Indo-Pacific Bottlenose Dolphins eat many fish and squid.

They live in oceans around India, Australia, Africa, and China.

 **J** is for a Jelly Fish

Mike Johnston © Wikimedia Commons

Jellies (jelly fish) kill their prey by stinging them.

They live in every ocean, and have been in the ocean for more than 500 million years.

 **K** is for a Killer Whale

Another name for a killer whale is an orca.

Killer whales have the seconded heaviest brain of any animal, it weighs over 12 pounds.

They are also smart animals, and humans train them to do tricks and shows.

L is for the Leafy Sea Dragon (Sea Horse)

dro!d © Wikimedia Commons

These types of seahorses have very good camouflage, since they look like the seaweed.

They live on the west and south coasts of Australia.

is for a Macaroni Penguin

Macaroni Penguins spend 3 out of every 4 hours in the ocean, this is where they are hunting for fish, krill, or squid to eat.

 **is for a Necklace Starfish**

Hectonichus © Wikimedia Commons

Necklace starfish are about 12 inches from one side to the other.

They live mostly in the Indian Ocean, and eat sponges, detritus, and other small sea creatures.

O
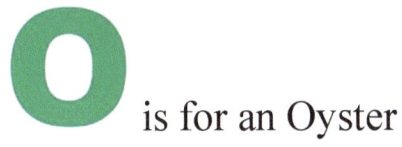
is for an Oyster

Many oysters have pearls inside, but most of them are not valuable.

A group of oysters is called a bed.

P is for a Puffer Fish

For defense a puffer fish will fill up with air or water, making themselves bigger.

They also have spines all over, so if bitten it will cut the predator's mouth.

 **Q** is for a Queensland Giant Grouper

Ginkgo100 © Wikimedia Commons

They live in the coral reefs around the coast of Australia, and are the largest bony fish to live there.

Giant Grouper can be as long as 9 feet and weigh as much as 880 pounds!

R is for the Red Crab

Red Crabs will lay their eggs on land, and then carry them on their bellies to float away into the ocean with the waves.

Red crabs have such a hard shell, they can pop car tires if ran over (the tire goes flat and the crab survives).

S is for a Shrimp

To hide from predators shrimp will jump up and dive onto the sandy ocean floor.

Shrimp are better at swimming than walking.

Shrimp is the #1 eaten seafood in the Unites States; we eat about 1 billion pounds per year.

T

is for a Tun Shell

James St. John © Wikimedia Commons

Tun shells belong to large sea snails.

These shells are thin, but very strong.

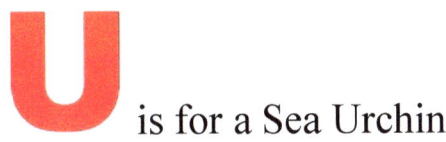 is for a Sea Urchin

The mouth of a sea urchin in the bottom, it has five hollow teeth inside.

They do not have eyes, their spins are very sensitive, and help them guide them.

V

is for a Vampire Squid

© Wikimedia Commons

They only live in very warm, tropical oceans throughout the World.

Instead of inking when predators, the vampire squid will released blue illuminating (lit up) mucus from their arms.

W is for a Whale

The heaviest animal on the planet is the sperm whale, weighing up to 70 ton!

Whales are found in all the oceans, but they like the Northern and Southern oceans the best, because they are colder.

X

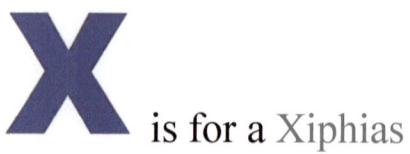 is for a Xiphias

Xiphias is the scientific name for a swordfish.

They do not use their "sword" nose to stab prey, they use it to slash them, like a real sword.

 is for a Yellowfin Tuna

Steve Evans © Wikimedia Commons

Yellowfin tuna travel in schools, sometimes with dolphins and whales.

They live mostly in the islands of the Pacific, especially around the Hawaiian Islands.

 is for Zooplankton

Matt Wilson/Jay Clark © <u>Wikimedia Commons</u>

Zooplanktons are tiny organisms that float in the ocean.

They are eaten by squid, bait fish, jelly fish, and they are a favorite of tuna.

Publisher

JD-Biz Corp

P O Box 374

Mendon, Utah 84325

http://www.jd-biz.com/

www.ingramcontent.com/pod-product-compliance
Lightning Source LLC
Chambersburg PA
CBHW050908290526
45792CB00002B/744